Telling Signs

poems by

Marvin J. Lurie

Finishing Line Press
Georgetown, Kentucky

Telling Signs

Copyright © 2023 by Marvin J. Lurie
ISBN 979-8-88838-072-7 First Edition
All rights reserved under International and Pan-American Copyright Conventions. No part of this book may be reproduced in any manner whatsoever without written permission from the publisher, except in the case of brief quotations embodied in critical articles and reviews.

Publisher: Leah Huete de Maines
Editor: Christen Kincaid
Cover Art: Ruby Hale
Author Photo: Max Pluenneke
Cover Design: Elizabeth Maines McCleavy

Order online: www.finishinglinepress.com
also available on amazon.com

Author inquiries and mail orders:
Finishing Line Press
P. O. Box 1626
Georgetown, Kentucky 40324
U. S. A.

Table of Contents

Telling Signs

On Finding Remnants of An Abandoned Farm Deep
    in the State Forest 1
Miriam's Well 2
Near the Headwaters of the Des Plaines River 3
Drinking with the Moon 4
Fishing 5
The Slough 6
The Baseline Road Bridge Was Washed Away 7
Fishing on the Sandy River 8
We Get Our Sailboat Ready for Summer 9
The Descendants 10
Rituals 11
In the Garden 12
Dream Walking 15
Footprints 16
House 17
I've Thought About You 18
Xerxes' Stone Mason 19
Telling Signs 20

Blood and Voices

Cain is Not Answered 23
Cain is Answered 24
The Birthright, According to Esau 25
Uriah 26
Joab, Prince of the Army 27
Grandpappy's War 28
Wilson Creek 30
At Burnside's Bridge 31
Sharpshooter 32
Sayler's Creek 34
The Empty Sleeve at Newport 35
Blood and Music 36

The Pillars of the World

When It Was Summer and I Was Young 41
What I Can Tell You 42
Companions 43
Timelines 44
What Went Right 45
Self-Portrait in Wool, Velvet and Buttons 47
The Undesirables 48
Field Surgeons, 1961 49
The Box Factory, 1955 50
Mr. Whitman Candles Eggs 51
Mr. Shumway's Cows 52
Earl, Jr.'s New Machine 53
Chinese Plate 54
Self-Portrait in Letters and Stones 55
A Tattered Coat Upon A Stick 57
Boxes 58
Unfinished Things 59
Mirror Mirror 60
The Pillars of the World 61

Acknowledgments 63
Notes 65
About the Author 67

*For my wife Sylvia,
first reader, critique and fan.*

Telling Signs

On Finding Remnants of An Abandoned Farm Deep in the State Forest

—Lu-shih

Praise the one who finds these stones.
He walks ground that keeps our bones.

He learns we stayed our days here
before pines scattered their cones

to conceal our hard-made fields,
where trees turn the winds to moans

that mourn not our failed farm,
Our labor, that time disowns.

Miriam's Well

> *Miriam died there and was buried there.*
> *The people were without water...*
> —Numbers 20:1, 2

You who were seeded by the stars,
what have you done?

Go to rivers that roar down frozen mountains.
Witness the fields of stones abandoned by their currents.

Go to where mountain tops are blasted into their valleys.
Breathe in the soot of their burning mud.

Go to the parched valleys and woodlands.
Feel the hot winds burn away forests.

Go to where winds search the headlands for passage.
Listen to them push aside the chains of the sea.

Miriam's well is falling farther and farther behind you.
What have you done with the garden that was given into your care?

Near the Headwaters of the Des Plaines River

The river is deep here, fast for a prairie stream.
It runs alongside a narrow marshy field
that can shuck off a boot.
I walk the solid edge.
My dog pushes into the brush to flush out a pheasant.
I swing my shotgun into the arc of its flight.
My shot tumbles the bird into the river.
My dog splashes across the field, jumps in after it.
She tries to climb out.
The bird in her mouth pushes against the high bank.
She falls back, drops it.
Swims downstream after it, twice.
The bird is pulled under by the current.
She struggles out, shakes herself off and comes to me.
I let go of my breath.
We walk to higher ground.
I sit on a stump with her next to me and watch the river.
Near here one spring, after the ice went out,
I saw a deer in the river
caught in tree roots under the bank.

Drinking with The Moon

I take my wine out to the garden
and raise my glass to the moon

as I often do. We are old friends.
She and my shadow make us three.

Two glasses and my worries vanish.
My shadow and I dance to celebrate

the dream of life. As if indifferent stars did not
foretell the moon and my shadow will abandon me.

Fishing

At dusk I was at the shore casting.
My lure, catching only glints of last light,
settled soundlessly
into the water. Leaves and twigs eddied,
pushed together against the shore,
some sank, some floated away.

We were all together in the same place once,
standing around a few branches burning on old ashes,
smoke mixing with our breaths,
waiting to start a hunt, as if some augury
about the best time could be divined
from how sparks rose in the filtered light,
one who died before we were ready,
one who is lost to us, adrift
somewhere, one who is not well
and waiting to leave,
and me. I don't hunt anymore.
I stand at the shore and cast.

The Slough

A low flat bridge, not much longer than wide,
hidden by grass, crossed the narrow end of the slough.

I stepped up on its dry platform to take in the rushes
and willow saplings lining the flow
and found an island in a world of barely seen shapes
slipping away underwater:

frogs escaping into hidden, watery paths,
the stare of a sculpture-still heron,
a silent blackbird swaying on the tallest cattail
over blue and white reflections.

The world slowly recovered
from the sudden sound of boots on wood,
from my long shadow and predator's scent.

The heron took a measured step.
The blackbird trilled
and flashed his scarlet shoulders.
Frogs came back to the shore.
Fish tailed back under the bridge.
A muskrat, swimming, turned to look at me,
as a commuter might
who sees something unusual beside the road
and turned back to its journey.

The Baseline Road Bridge Was Washed Away

The river is a stone's-throw across here.
It runs clear in sunlight.

You can see concrete rubble from the piers.
Rust marks where iron struts melted away,
trail streamers of green algae.

Cement on the fragments is washing away,
smoothing the edges,
releasing sand and gravel into the riverbed.

Stand here in the afternoon.

The current will lull you.
The air will waver with swarms of midges.
The sun will set over the willows,
lining the road across the river,
coloring the leaves golden.

If you want to go there,
you will have to find another way.

Fishing on the Sandy River

Churning flow pushes against my waders.
The glacier-fed river urges me to, *come along.*

Its faceted current scatters light.
Flickers of sun beguile me to, *come along.*

Restive water whispers in my ears,
entices me to, *come along.*

Sighing wind escorts the river through the canyon,
presses against me, encourages me to, *come along.*

Join my escape from the mountain, the river says.
Travel with me to the great sea, come along.

Firs grasping the rock walls of the canyon,
the otter sunning on the far bank,
together they say,
stay with us, stay with us.

We Get Our Sailboat Ready for Summer

The three of us sat on overturned
five-gallon buckets on the dock
watching the river.

The brownish gray water was choppy.
Across, a grassy marsh.
Far off, an oil refinery flared methane.

We had scraped, caulked and painted all day in the sun,
finished all the beer.
Our radio's batteries ran down and quit.
Our shirts were spattered with copper bottom paint.
Brushes soaked in coffee cans filled with gasoline.
Mist and dusk settled over the river.

I was thinking about the previous summer on the boat,
the parties, the women,
tried to remember names and bodies,
connect them to weekends and harbors,
got confused and started over.

I didn't know this would be our last summer together on the water.

The Descendants

Morning. Snow high enough to hide traffic on the county road.
I unplug the oil heater
and pound on the hood of the truck
to warn the cats sleeping next to the engine block.

Lean scavengers with scarred muzzles
and half-bitten-off ears,
they forage in fields and yards,
snarl and hiss when rousted.

Descendants of refugees from development,
who migrated here when this place offered bovine warmth,
ample rodents, occasional fish heads
or bowls of old bread soaked in milk
and they were valued workers.
Now the barn sells second hand goods.
Cats patrol the edges,
make do with pilfered scraps,
unwary birds, field mice
and little charity.

They're often in the corner of my eye
scanning the yard from the under the porch,
stalking the fence line brush.
When I look right at them they slip away.
No one will take them in.
And they will not be taken in.

Rituals

A few roses hold back summer colors
long after leaves have clogged the rain gutters.
My wife is making fried green tomatoes
from those that started too late.
Their floured slices
look like our snow covered lawn.
What has not been laid in for winter
will not be.

We once raised a goose for this season.
All summer he patrolled the frontiers of our yard
and only stood down to eat the corn we gave him.
I still remember that goose,
how he looked in my eyes when I came for him.
Together we entered that ancient ritual:
death given, death to be received.

In the Garden

    I.   **Lives**

Why do you sit on hard rocks by the river
and think the roiling current makes you immortal
when you can see swirling past all the other lives?

Go to the edge of the water at sunrise. Listen
to the geese calling. Let your feet get wet with dew. Tell me
why you say the geese flying away tell us our lives?

Bring me a teaspoon of morning mist. Tell me
how many raindrops there are. Teach me
to hear a rainbow singing and the wind that foretells our lives.

You saw strangers on the road and called to them
but they did not stop. They were hurrying
to the next brighter thing. They were our lives.

I looked for you at the circus parade,
but the clowns and acrobats lured you away.
You ran after them shouting to be let into their lives.

If you come back in spring, I will come out to meet you
in the garden. We can read our futures in the clouds,
at night listen to the Pleiades tell us our lives.

    II.   **Gates**

If you come back in summer, you must find your way
through thickets and walled gardens
on a winding dusty road, opening and closing gates.

Wind is the earth's prophet, dust its prophecy.
I will wash the dust from your feet with cool water
to refresh you from your journey, opening and closing gates.

To the sun you are a shadow,
to the moon a reflection walking
through dream after dream, opening and closing gates.

You will see a man who can only walk
in one direction. If you call out to him,
he will keep on walking, opening and closing gates.

The man is leading people to the next place.
No one can come back from there. They are hurrying
to keep up with him, opening and closing gates.

Turn away from the man who only walks in one direction.
If you become lost, I will come out on the road
to find you, opening and closing gates.

III.   You

If you come back through the snow in winter
follow the smoke from my fire.
I will come out to the garden gate when I see you.

The sun and the moon are my companions.
Their long winter shadows slide across the snow
to mark the short days and long nights 'till I see you.

Shadow is the sun's servant, time its burden
carried endless days from dawn to dusk. Its arc
will strand you in the night and I will never see you.

Do not believe the night sky. Its restless stars are dreams
from before time to turn you around and back.
If you follow them, I will never see you.

Everything is burning. Our lives melt away
and the dark rushes in. Sit in the light of my fire.
Time burns more slowly when I see you.

Dawn will shatter crystal on burnished snow.
Winter Annas will blaze rubies and emeralds,
gifts from the garden when I see you.

      IV.   **Walls**

Come back through the forest in spring.
I will sit with you in the garden. We will listen to the fountain,
watch the sun pull its shadow over the garden walls.

The moon will dress the statues in silver.
Hold out your hands. They will fill with silver.
Silver will flow down the garden walls.

In spring there will be flowers and sweet grass,
in summer honey and cool nights, in fall apples and red wine,
in winter you will be safe within the garden walls.

The moon is just the moon. The world
will not be healed while we watch the seasons.
Its sorrows will press against the garden walls.

Tell me stories from the forest of sorrows.
Sing me its songs. Teach me secret trails
to the world beyond the garden walls.

For the forest will grow in on us.
Shadows will veil the statues and fountain.
Darkness will drive us from the garden walls.

Dream Walking

On my walk this morning,
thinking about a recently lost friend,
the woods opened to a field I hadn't seen before
choked with purple loosestrife.

A wood frame house,
paint long since sanded off by wind,
windows broken out, doors gone,
stood alone in the field.

I stepped up on the porch,
touched the door frame,
sensed its nails strain and grumble.
The house would not let them go,

and they were no longer proud of their work.
They sent me to the empty front room,
walls decorated by a gallery of water stains
like portraits of ancestors

whose stories were forgotten.
Their faces turned toward the back doorway
where I could see a dried dirt yard
with a rust-flaked standing pump,

its long handle worn smooth with use.
Beside it an empty bucket for water to prime the pump.
If I went to the back door,
the faces would be looking through it,

telling me to go out.
The field beyond was lost in a blaze of sun
so bright it darkened my vision.
I decided not to go there today.

Footprints

Australopithecus Afarensis

You who were not yet us,
who shared this upright conceit,
who left these footprints in mud that dried to stone,
were you thinking your view to the horizon was mastery—
that you could envision a future—
that your children would outlive you?

If you bequeathed these thoughts to us, they endured.
We used them for certain things,
some of them good. Now we chip at ancient rock,
name fragments of ancestors, try to uncover the line
that tells our descent from you.

Our horizon is the sky, our immortality
bright metal with writings we send toward the stars
looking for others,
looking for the place where our footprints might survive
for an unimaginable future when time has swallowed us too.

House

Enclosed in my errand,
I step on the stair that squeaks.
It's the scratchy voice of the house
reminding me of its virtues,
saying, *Attend to me.*
I am old but secure. My walls
need Spackle in some places
but they keep out the wind and rain
and will never let your furniture
slip out onto the lawn.
My windows look out
on trees and flowers in summer
and can be closed to the cold in winter.
The furnace grumbles in the basement,
but it can be replaced.
I will always be your house.

I move my foot and the house
seems satisfied.
It goes back to its shelterly jobs
until the next time I am distracted
and forget.

I've Thought About You

I read about your children's charity in the paper.
I thought you would do something socially useful,
you grieved so for the world.

You haven't married, which doesn't surprise me.
You skittered away from commitment
like a filly shying away from a glittering stone in her path.

You were going to spend the summer
learning to play The Well-Tempered Clavier
and not come out at all,
but were aroused thinking about us together
and would sneak away
to be with me.

You were lithe and elusive behind a veil of black hair,
so I'm surprised at how round and contented you look in the picture.
You must have needed a long solitude
unhindered by intimacy
for that contentment to flower.

After more than fifty years,
I still have the small ivory Buddha you gave me
to send me away.
It has been moved to a lesser space
in a seldom-used room.
When I see it,
I think about you.

Xerxes' Stone Mason

—Seen at the Oriental Institute, University of Chicago

I don't know your name,
only your mark:
two point-to-point reclining diamonds
hidden in the design
claiming an arm's-length piece of gray stone lintel
with its frieze of standing lions
chiseled for the coming in and going out of Xerxes.

But I can see you from here,
in a dusty work yard under the Persian sun
surrounded by piles of uncut stone.
You have a leather apron and palm pads
fight hard stone with soft iron,
eat your lunch of lentils, rice, and flatbread,
trade the rough humor and banter of laborers.

I want to tell you,
the palaces of Xerxes are pulled down,
their pieces collected and displayed in museums,
but your mark survives, declares
the hard work of building empires
is done with hammers, chisels and sweat,
by proud builders who mark their work.

Telling Signs

Fall weekends
my dog and I escaped the city early
for fields and hedgerows.

I relive those sharp mornings,
the painted dawns,
walking through brush in boots,
the heft and balance of my shotgun,
the good shots and retrieves,
how we worked together,
telling signs back and forth in our own ways.

Retired from the field, we took long walks,
discovered a new wilderness,
retrieved sticks in new waters,
explored overgrown trails.
Colors flowed from green to amber
to winter sere to green.
Walks became shorter
until she was content
with the living room rug and back yard
as her whole world.

I think she too relived
the beauty and perfection of those days
in running dreams.

Blood and Voices

Cain is Not Answered

Let there be hatred and strife,
conquest and rebellion.
There is no justice.

I am not sent among men as a sign
against blood vengeance.

I am the messenger of murder without end.

From this day to the end of the world
there will be no reward for the righteous,
no punishment for the wicked.

I have been an obedient son, suffered
to plow the reluctant earth
to atone for my parents' transgression.

Still, I am denied honor by my brother's
favor before God. Why am I tested so?
I will go into the world!

There I will breed a race of armorers.
My sons will spread the message of silence
against murder. They will proclaim:

There is no justice and no judge,
no world-to-come. There will be war forever.

Cain is Answered

Cain the aggrieved was a farmer
in a tribe of nomadic herders
suspicious of settlements and tillers of the soil.

He was enraged by the injustice,
assaulted his brother with harsh words.
Abel was arrogant and prideful.
The well-known event occurred.

Modern Cain was involved in a drive-by.
Unlike his biblical ancestor, he had a lawyer
who claimed he was only a passenger.
Cain was back on the street in 25 months.

Our Cain had a jailhouse conversion,
opened a store-front mission,
counseled addicts and street kids,
preached in shelters, found jobs for hookers.
Business for dealers and pimps suffered.
They ordered the hit that put down Cain.

In his last moments, Cain understood
his parable had expired.

The Birthright, According to Esau

Oh stars. Oh stars, my roof, my tent.
The whole earth is my support
and the sky is my shelter.
It covers me when I lie down to rest.
Like the wild fruit and the olive tree
that flourish in both sun and rain,
I take my strength from the land.
I am as the lion, lord of the hills and forests.
I feast on the fat of the earth.
The morning dew is my prayer and my blessing.
As the rutting beasts of the field obey creation's plan,
so do the lives of men.
So it is that I am of the earth where all is one,
creation and creator.
I am in the stone and tree.
I am one with the ram and red cattle.
The sun and the moon are my ancestors.
Everything is given to me and nothing taken away.

Uriah

> *King David wrote, "Place Uriah in the front lines*
> *where the fighting is fiercest;*
> *then fall back so he may be killed."*
> *—2 Samuel: 11.15*

Beneath the battlements of Rabbah,
embraced in the arms of our regiment
my comrades and I, who accept our fate,
have written our wills, unbound our widows.

I have honored my soldier's oath,
left the arms of Bathsheba
to carry a sword for my king.

Now my loyalty is repaid by treachery
so shameless it cannot be hidden,
my wife and my life taken from me.

Thus do kings shatter the lives of those they entangle.

Even so, I will go willingly with my brothers
into the unknown
for that has always been our destination.

Oh my David, may the sword never depart from your house.

Joab, Prince of the Army

> *King David said to Solomon, "So act in accordance with your wisdom and see that his white hair does not go down to Sheol in peace."*
> —*1 Kings: 2.5*

I am a soldier.
I fought where I was sent and won where I fought.

As the walls of a city sit on solid stone,
the house of David rests on my victories.

I have destroyed nations to defend God's commandments
and held His statutes higher than the designs of kings.

Now I grasp the horns of the altar in the tent of the Lord,
as I once gripped the handle of my sword

with the strength given to me by Him
to crush the wickedness of our enemies,

and appeal to Him for justice.
That I have slain killers, rebels and traitors

is not murder. Yet
the hand of my king reaches out from his grave

to order my execution
even in this holy place.

Generations will know how David repaid loyalty.
Guilt will stain his house for this sacrilege.

Eternity will curse his line with disease, poverty and war
for as long as it bears sons.

Grandpappy's War

The little ones keep asking,
how come I've only two fingers and a thumb
on my left hand? I made up a story.

I reached down to grab a fish off my hook.
Another fish must have thought my fingers were worms

because it jumped up and bit them off.
Truth is, on July 21, 1861
I was with the 1st Massachusetts and Colonel Codwin,
right at the end of my ninety-day enlistment,
not eager to get shot at.

We spent the day marching back and forth
behind the lines,
got moved from the 1st to 5th Division in reserve,
watched the fighting around Bull Run Creek,
happy to be out of it.

Late afternoon our soldiers ran back from the fight;
some of them threw away their packs and rifles.

We were ordered down to the front to keep back the Rebels
who seemed just as muddled. Some cannon shots
discouraged them from coming after us,
but not before I saw two of our fellows shot down.

The road back to Centreville was jammed with a jumble of soldiers, wagons
and carriages of people who came to picnic and watch the battle,
everyone trying to push through the crowd.

The wheel of a caisson I was helping push slipped off the road
knocked me down with the wheel on my hand and crushed my fingers.
That ended my afternoon of war.

The gun Sargent tore strips from my shirt to bind me up and stop me bleeding.
In Washington a doctor gave me a canteen with hard liquor,
a leather strap to bite on
and nipped off my fingers.

That was enough war for me, so I came home.
I'll tell anyone about the fish, though.

Wilson Creek

Orderly Sargent Brackett with Colonel T. J. Churchill,
1st. Arkansas Mounted Riflemen, August 10, 1861 Wilson Creek, MO

There were bodies all over the fields and ravines
after the Yankees retreated.
We watched our division surgeon, Dr. Smith,
and the Union doctor walk the battlefield
to sort the wounded from the dead.
Our General Pierce came and led the Union doctor
to where they'd brought Union General Lyon's body in a wagon.

I saw Lyon shot from his horse.
We were hiding in thick brush at the edge of a ravine.
Some Iowa and Kansas companies
charged right at us with bayonets,
Lyon in front waving his hat.

When Pierce asked for volunteers
to escort Lyon's body to Springfield,
 I thought it was right to go.
At home we would always
bring a man's body to his family.

Yankee soldiers stood at attention and saluted
when we drove by their camp with the wagon.
One army camp
can look like any other one.

We were quiet
riding back to our regiment.

At Burnside's Bridge

> *It was no longer alone the boom of the batteries, but a rattle of musketry—*
> *at first like pattering drops upon a roof; then a roll, crash, roar, and rush,*
> *like a mighty ocean billow upon the shore, chafing the pebbles, wave*
> *on wave, with deep and heavy explosions of the batteries, like the crashing*
> *of the thunderbolts.*
> —Charles Carleton Coffin, Army Correspondent

It was a September afternoon,
cloudy, mild and humid.
Leaves had started to fall.
This slow flat creek, waist deep,
only a pistol shot across.
This stone bridge, with three arches,
solid and reliable,
could hold a small cannon rolling across,
deflect enemy bullets.
I was killed here that afternoon.
My body floated downstream to the Potomac,
never found.
You won't find my name either
on any lists of the 23,000 casualties
because I wasn't an officer. Just another Yankee private
in the 51st New York Regiment with Colonel Potter.
I could fire my Springfield Musket three times a minute,
kill Johnny Reb from 200 yards.
But that day we were just across from each other,
Rebels on that rocky bank over there.
Us on the road along this side.
They killed us all afternoon from behind those rocks
until we rolled a howitzer onto the bridge,
blew them away with double canister
and charged across.
That's when I got hit and fell into the water.
There's no plaque or marker right here.
That's why I'm telling you about the day I was killed
on the bridge over Antietam Creek.

Sharpshooter

Father wasn't much for farming.
My brothers doing the work.
He'd sit in the woods, his back to a tree,
long rifle across his knees,
sharing his lunch biscuits with the birds.

Most days he'd bring home meat for the pot.
I was his youngest.
As soon as I could sit still he'd take me along.
I was of a generally quiet nature
so it suited me.

When I was almost tall as the rifle, he taught me to load and shoot it.
It wasn't long before I could hit a squirrel in the eye at 100 paces.
That's how I came to be a sharpshooter
at Pittsburgh Landing an early morning in April, '62
high in a tree
watching some Rebels unlimber their cannons.

They were so far away
they didn't seem more than uniforms.

I waited until one brought his gun around
and shot him.
An officer spotted my smoke with his glass.
One of their guards tried to get a bead on me.
I put him down too.

By then there were three big muzzles pointed my way
so I scrambled into the woods behind me.
I dodged Rebel pickets most of the afternoon.
One spotted me and got a shot off
but only splattered me with tree bark.
I still have a mark on my cheek.
At dusk I caught up and made camp
with my brigade.

At first light I filled my canteen,
stuffed biscuits in my pockets
and looked for a likely spot.

After the war I came home to try farming.
But like my father,
I'd rather sit in the woods,
my back to a tree,
my rifle across my knees.
I try to write down my thoughts about the war,
but the words jumble.

Sayler's Creek

The boots I took off a dead Yankee in December
are worn clear through, stuffed with rags.

We marched four days and nights,
two with no food,
and shot up the Union center at Sayler's Creek.

Me and my fellows,
we were not beat.

We should have held out until dark,
escaped through the woods.
Instead, I was a Union prisoner yesterday,
free today without an army.

I fought four years with General Ewell.
Now I'm 300 miles from my home
in Columbia, South Carolina.

I'm looking to pick up a musket,
some powder and shot to feed myself
and walk home.

A Union soldier gave me some hardtack and sowbelly to take along.

The Empty Sleeve at Newport

The war continues working, day and night...accustoms young women to waiting.
  —*The War Works Hard*, Dunya Mikhail

A shadow follows their leisure at the shore
darkens the left side of their faces.
They ride in an open, two-wheel trap,
wicker sides and fenders, plush cushions.

She has a slender waist,
a riding hat, its ribbons streaming behind her.
Puffed sleeves lead to delicate hands
that control the reins and whip,
as she leans into the motion of the horse.
Wide eyes serious about her new role, this unfamiliar independence.

He wears a fashionable waistcoat, collared shirt, small tie,
the empty left sleeve of his jacket pinned inside its lapel,
a Union army campaign cap.

He is pensive. His world has changed.
A woman drives his horse-drawn trap with confident hands.

Blood and Music

"Two thousand songs were published
in the first year of the Civil War."
Some of the tunes enlisted
in both the South and North.

In the first year of the Civil War
Mother I'm Coming Home to Die was sung
by both the South and North
and *Dixie* was first a Northern song.

Mother I'm Coming Home to Die,
We Shall Meet But We Shall Miss Him,
and *Dixie* that was first a Northern song
were sung in music halls and homes.

We Shall Meet But We Shall Miss Them
they answered the *Battle Cry of Freedom*
sung in music halls and homes
and spilled their blood for the Union.

They answered the *Battle Cry of Freedom*
and died for the *Bonnie Blue Flag*
or spilled their blood for the Union
as they marched to the *Federal Eagle.*

They died for the *Bonnie Blue Flag*
or sang *We Are Coming Father Abraham 300,000 More*
as they marched to the *Federal Eagle*
dying to undo that great wrong.

We Are Coming Father Abraham 300,000 More.
Tramp, Tramp, Tramp the Boys Are Marching
dying to undo that great wrong.
But Johnny wouldn't be coming home again.

Tramp, Tramp, Tramp The Boys Were Marching
to all of the songs that were published.
but Johnny wouldn't be coming home again
To any to any of those marching tunes.

The Pillars of the World

When It Was Summer and I Was Young

roaring surf sang me to sleep.
It was the song of the beach and the waves:

Sleep. The stars are safe in the heavens.
Dream of the day just past and the next.
The trees and the fields in the sun,
the dunes and the grasses
will remember you and welcome you.
No one can love you the way we do.

What I Can Tell You

It's not like Rodin's Gates
or the Bosch Damned.
You will never see flames,
as is commonly thought.
It is more like a heavy fog.
You will walk through that fog forever.
You will hear unintelligible voices.
But if you walk toward those voices,
they will recede from you.

Did I say,
there is no furniture?

Companions

We never grow tired of each other,
my shadow and I.

We welcome the sun as companion,
a party of three friends.

We wander and idle together,
imbibe sweet spring air,

savor summer's heat,
toast fall's blaze of leaves,

mourn the shortness of winter light.
My shadow and I journey 10,000 miles

under the sun.
My shadow retires at the end of day.

I sit on the bench in a dark garden,
my cap beside me.

The moon hides behind clouds.
Shadows of shadows.

Timelines

My searches for the woman I could have married
find no more entries.

Somewhere there is a daughter
who might be mine.
She's probably a grandmother,
or great grandmother now.
That's how young we were then.

I've lost families I never had—
the arc of their fierce young lives,
the daily awareness of their presence.

The sky is growing light.
I can see bushes and trees in the garden.
I'm going out soon to mulch the flower beds.

What Went Right

Old wooden Chicago "L" cars on the Ravenswood line
had open platforms at each end
that I rode to my after-school job.

In the clang and crash of slamming side to side,
shrieking rail curves,
rattling clatter of joints and switches—
one hand for the black iron railings,
one for a cigarette—I practiced belonging
to the community of men
who worked the second shift.

It's where I learned to wear denim jackets,
plaid flannel shirts and jeans
bought from push carts on Maxwell Street.
I studied apartment windows and porches flashing by
to spy on the lives of people who lived with their backs
to the "L" tracks,
their kitchen tables, shirts and underwear hung out to dry,
geranium pots on railings and stairs,
old women watching the trains.

I showed off my one-handed trick
of lighting "strike anywhere" Diamond matches
for my unfiltered Pall Malls,
scraping my thumbnail across their sulfur tips.

I learned that from Abe,
a rough old teamster, squat and thick-armed,
who drove a horse-drawn milk wagon when he was fifteen
and grew up on the west side
with guys who became made men.
He had a furniture store,
liked to ride his trucks, stay out of the office.
He'd sleep in the corner of the cab
with a dead Dutch Masters cigar clamped in his teeth,
let me, "the kid," drive the Studebaker.

He'd wake up, tell me stories.
He rode the rails during the depression.
The mobster in the headlines was a nasty punk
who stole milk from his wagon.
He'd do that trick with a match, take a few puffs,
fall asleep again.

He taught me to carry heavy dressers and mattresses
up three flights of stairs,
to load every bit of space in a truck,
saying, *Don't do this, kid.*
Get an education. Wear a suit and tie.
He made me his helper to open a new store,
to tear down walls, build new ones,
run power and plumbing, lay floors.

He taught me to keep at it until a job was done,
and that a good way to end a day's work
was to have a cigar, a mug of black coffee
with a shot of Old Grandad bourbon stirred in
and talk about what went right.

Self-Portrait in Wool, Velvet and Buttons

Few tangibles survive:
a black and white photo
of serious-looking people wearing elegant clothes.
You can't tell:
my grandmother had been a great beauty,
my grandfather was gentle and caring.
You can't tell:
the stylish, wool coat my three-year-old self is wearing,
with its double-breasted rows of buttons
and velvet collar,
was hand cut and sewn by him.,

I have the picture and the coat
waiting in a closet

for me to become
like my grandfather,
an image in a picture looking at the future,
for another generation to be told
my grandfather made a coat for me by hand.
My grandmother was beautiful.

The Undesirables

> *They caused the outbreak of thieving and robbery all over the country.*
> —Henry Ford

One bookkeeper.
Two school teachers.
Two lawyers.
One marketing professional.
Two small business owners.
A trade association executive.
The descendants so far of Rebekah and Jacob the tailor.*
who came in 1905.
Their good fortune.
The US Congress soon decided they were undesirables.
There were too many of them.
We couldn't accept any more. Or at least not many.
They didn't speak English and wouldn't eat our food.
They lived in slums and had too many children.
They worked cheap and pushed down wages.
They weren't real Americans.
And, of course, they were Christ-killers.
Millions were left behind.
Jacob's younger sister, her husband and daughter,
were taken out of their home and shot down in the street
by the Einsatzgruppen.

*My grandparents

Field Surgeons, 1961

I came down out of the mountains at dusk
with a respiratory infection.

Burt and I wandered the streets of Vienna,
eventually found a doctor missing
his left hand and forearm
alone in an all-night clinic
in the front room of a private home.

We talked symptoms with our
almost German, his almost English,
laughed at being unable to understand
a word in either language for diarrhea.

He recognized our names were Jewish.
He said he once had many Jewish patients
in his orthopedic practice.

He had been an army field surgeon in the war.
When he was wounded, Americans took care of him.
The Jewish field surgeon who took off his hand
said he felt bad he had to do it
but there was no way to save it.

After a penicillin shot and some pills
he helped me count out the small payment in coins.
The three of us sat for a while
looking out the front windows
at people on the sidewalk,
got up together
as if there had been an agreement.

The Box Factory, 1955

I can see it in his eyes, this is his life.
I'm the honky college kid about to mess with it.

We're on opposite sides of a steel worktable,
making olive drab quart-sized boxes.
We take stacks of cardboard sheets off the cutting press,
three rows of four boxes, break them apart,
pound off scrap with ball peen hammers.
He shows off his power by taking huge handfuls.
I work faster with smaller stacks,
keep the delivery rack from piling up so high
even he can't handle the load.
By lunch I earn a lesser degree of resentment.

We hammer, sweat, trash talk,
fill skids with flat boxes
for six weeks,
buck twenty-five an hour, 8 to 4:30,
half hour lunch, two 10-minute breaks,
machines grind and clatter around us
on their own schedules.
I get a broken-toothed grin
when we work fast enough to get ahead of the press
to take a seconds-long break.
I just keep thinking,
five more weeks,
four more weeks,
three more weeks...
and I'm out of here with school money,
leave him to his life.

Mr. Whitman Candles Eggs

This morning for breakfast
I took two eggs from the fridge.
Holding them in my hand
I was struck by the whiteness around me:
white eggs, white fridge, white stove, white sink, white dishwasher,
how unnatural it all seemed.

Our eggs were brown
when I stayed with my grandmother during summers.
We bought them from the Whitman's
who had a farm stand on the highway.

Sometimes I sat on their cellar steps
and watched Mr. Whitman candle that morning's eggs.
He had cut the bottom off a tin funnel
turned it over a light bulb on a wire frame like a shade
and rolled each egg over the bulb
so they glowed from inside
to reveal any cracks or blood spots.
Those couldn't be sold.

On hot days I think about that cool cellar,
its field stone walls and jumble
of no longer used tools and implements.
And I look at yard sales and in antique stores
for a hand made tin candler like Mr. Whitman's
to keep in my kitchen.
It should be rusted and dented
and look out of place.

Mr. Shumway's Cows

Listing, sun-bleached posts
of what was once a fence
run alongside what was once a road,
drunkenly hold up a memory of wire,
keep the ghosts of Mr. Shumway's cows
from wandering into the backyards
that were once a corn field.

Slantwise, I can still see those furrows,
the gravel road.

And here comes my grandfather
walking down that road holding my hand.

We're going to buy a bottle of milk from Mr. Shumway.

Something is wrong today.
Mr. Shumway is shaking his head,
pointing to his cows, waving his hand at the corn.
I understand *no more milk*.
No more walks here holding my grandfather's hand

My grandfather is a thin man with soft hands.
He comes out from the city
to read me stories and take me for walks.
He explains that Mr. Shumway is moving away.
People are coming to build houses.

Walking back, I hold my grandfather's hand
really tight.

Earl, Jr.'s New Machine

We liked to watch Earl Whitman candle eggs,
two skinny boys tired of summer sun
allowed to sit in his cool stone cellar
as long as we were quiet.

He bent over his homemade tin and light bulb candler,
the cords on the back of his hands
pulling his fingers back and forth
on a fixed path
from wire baskets to candler to egg cartons
one egg at a time
without ever hesitating or slowing down.

This morning I stopped at the Whitman Food Market.
Earl, Jr. (except he's dropped the Jr.)
took me in back to see his new machine,
as big as a pool table,
that grades and sorts eggs.
He said that with almost 1,000 hens
it's what he needs to keep up.
He keeps his Dad's tin candler on his desk, he said.
When worries about so many chickens get too heavy,
it relaxes him to turn it over in his hands.

Chinese Plate

It's always spring on the Chinese plate
on my shelf. Willows on the pond have turned half-green.
A cluster of jonquils rises from its reflection,
boldly yellow in the fresh greens of spring.
A young woman, her dress decorated with plum blossoms,
sits in a bamboo pavilion
her hand raised, beckoning me to come closer,
sit ever beside her in this ever spring.

But I'll get bored there, restless, complain
 I want to explore the other side of the pond.
We'll argue. *That's not part of the deal,*
she'll say. *Time will start up again in my world.
I will grow old and undesirable.
You will leave me and go back to your world unchanged.*

I will leave now, I'll say. *I promise to come back
to enjoy spring with you for just a few minutes,
every day in every season.*

That's what I do. I slip out of my world
to sit with a beautiful woman on a beautiful spring day
for just a few minutes
every day in every season.

Self-Portrait in Letters and Stones

When we moved away, I bought Endowed Care
for my parents' and grandparents' graves.
I didn't want them vandalized by time
as so many graves there:
headstones tumbled,
overgrown by bushes and vines.
Many are for immigrants
who came knowing they would never again see their families,
the graves of their ancestors.
Now themselves abandoned.

I discard the past, unprepared
for what might well up years later
to demand closure.

In my mother's apartment after the funeral,
I found letters from my father
saved from before they married, I was born and he fled into death.

They burned my hand.
I threw them away unread,
my last chance to know my father.

Kongzi said when your parents have become ancestors,
they are still your parents.
Bury them and sacrifice to them
in accordance with the rites.

I relinquished my responsibility to the cemetery foundation
and its workers, who trim the grass, blow away leaves
and straighten headstones. I want to believe
they think about the dead in their care.

On their Day of the Dead they include
my ancestors in their prayers
so no one is abandoned.
On that day, I would reread my father's letters,

to know the man he was and if I'm like him,
settle with myself whether I have been worthy or not.
But nothing is ever settled.
It's too late.
It was always too late.

A Tattered Coat Upon A Stick

On its rounds the wind returns.
—Ecclesiastes: 1.6

Scarecrow's coat has no buttons.
It opens to the wind,
shows no heart,
only old clothes
that once warmed a living heart.

Scarecrow turns one way, then another,
with the ever-turning wind,
dawn to dawn in every season
showing he has no heart to every direction.

One passing by may see his own portion
in the open coat,
worn in both gladness and sorrow,
and see he is enmeshed in the net of time
and must do all he can.

For he cannot know when the sun, moon and stars
will go dark for him
and the wind grow quiet.

Boxes

I have become expert with boxes.
One with unopened shampoo
and hand cream for the shelter.

Another with still good sweaters and coats,
folded carefully, for Goodwill.

The one with a pitcher and glasses
wrapped and packed with crumpled newspaper
to a cousin who might use them.

A nicked and scratched kitchen table
taken apart, created and shipped to a brother.

Some necklaces, rings, and bracelets
to be parceled out to my family women.

Pictures divided and mailed to grandchildren.

A box of dishes to sit on a shelf,
too heavy with memories
to be taken down and used.

Each move yields more boxes,
until there is just a reclining chair,

a small table with a wedding picture and clock radio
in a narrow room with a single bed.

And I begin to fold flat and put aside
more cardboard boxes.

Unfinished Things

On the road out of town,
past the last straggle of houses,
each more disheveled than the last,
as if town-ness
dissipates at the edges
so houses are scattered
and roads wander from their grid,
there is a cement pad and stack
of prefab roof trusses,
weathered and gray from winters and summers
sitting out uncovered.

Someone meant to build something.
Whatever energy inspired his plan
petered out past the edge of town.

You find unfinished things at that border
where people don't cross over
into what might happen.
Over there is a revealing light.
Ghosts can cast shadows
of the past. Hidden selves
can be exposed.

Mirror Mirror

Good morning old man.
You no longer look like your grandfather
who never lived this long,
who became a gaunt skull and shriveled limbs

barely discernible beneath the heavy comforter
that gave neither comfort nor warmth to his wasting body.

Who no longer made me oatmeal in the morning
or peeled oranges to look like flowers on a plate.

Instead, I fed him in the evening from the tip of a flat wooden spoon
that came with the cup of ice cream I bought
with my nickel allowance.

One morning I found him, mouth and eyes open,
a trail of dark drool down his cheek.
I fell from life before into life after.

I was unmoored.

The Pillars of The World

There was a man who cut the hay around
my grandpa's summer place. He ruled a huge
machine. At his command it roared and sliced
and sent out mysteries of tractor smells,
exhaust and gas, hot oil and metal.
Only the greatest man could wield such power.

Each time the tractor man would cut the hay,
he cut the lot beside my grandpa's house
even though it mostly was just weeds.
When he was done, my grandpa would take down
two shot glasses and a bottle of schnapps,
and set the glasses on a tractor tire,
and pour them shots and talk about how
the world was made and what would happen next.

Acknowledgments

Brick and Mortar Review:
    "Fishing", "The Slough", "Rituals", and "Unfinished Things" (2nd Place Winner, 2005 Brick and Mortar Poetry Contest)

Spring into Poetry Journal:
    "The Pillars of the World" (Winner, 2001 Rosemary Sazonoff Creative Writing Contest)

Terra Incognita (anthology):
    "Miriam's Well"

The Covfefe Resistance (chapbook):
    "The Undesirables"

Verseweavers:
    "The Birthright, According to Esau" (Finalist, 2008 Oregon Poetry Association Contest)
    "On Finding Remnants of An Abandoned Farm Deep in the State Forest" (Winner, 2005 Oregon Poetry Association Contest)
    "Xerxes' Stone Mason" (Winner, 2010 Oregon Poetry Association Contest)

I owe thanks to the people who guided me on my adventures in poetry. Pattiann Rogers kick started my journey after a long hiatus. Ruth L. Schwartz and Vern Rutsala shed further light on my path. A special thanks to David Biespiel who during my years of participation in The Attic Institute of Arts and Letters as a member of the Poets Studio and a Fellow of the Atheneum has been teacher, coach, critic and friend; also to Wendy Willis of the Institute. Constance Hall and Steve Williams hosted a monthly critique group for many years that consistently helped me improve my writing. Thanks also to John Sibley Williams who helped me by editing and assembling this book. The poetry community in Oregon is a warm and welcoming collection of interesting people. Come join us.

Notes

"Grandpappy's War": This was the first battle of the Civil War and the first time these soldiers were in combat. This is the experience of an actual unit and its colonel.

"Wilson Creek": Union Brigadier General Nathaniel Lyon was the first general killed in the Civil War. Although he was outnumbered and defeated, his quick action in challenging the Confederate advance neutralized the effectiveness of the pro-Southern forces in Missouri allowing the Union forces to secure the state for the Union.

"At Burnside's Bridge": Antietam was the bloodiest day in US history before or since. It was Lee's first attempt to invade the North. There was no clear victor, but Lee chose to withdraw from Maryland across the Potomac to Virginia. In military terms he had conceded the field of battle so it was considered a Union victory. This gave Lincoln the political space to issue the Emancipation Proclamation and ended the agitation in England and France to recognize the Confederacy as an independent country.

"Sayler's Creek": On a windy February 17, 1865 half to two thirds of Columbia, S.C. was destroyed by fire. It was set by Union Soldiers sacking the city.

"The Empty Sleeve at Newport": Poem is after an illustration by Winslow Homer, for a story in Harper's Weekly, August 26, 1865.

"Blood and Music": The sentence "Two thousand songs were published in the first year of the Civil War." is a sentence repeated in several books on Civil War Music.

"On Finding Remnants of An Abandoned Farm Deep in the State Forest": Lu-shih is Vietnamese. It is related to an ancient form of Chinese poetry that became established at the end of the 7th Century. It came into Vietnamese literature during China's long domination of Vietnam and became established as a traditional Vietnamese form. Lu-shih is both syllabic and rhymed. It consists of four couplets of seven syllable lines, with the first, second, fourth, sixth and eighth lines rhymed.

ABOUT THE AUTHOR

Marvin J. Lurie is a retired trade association executive who lives in Portland, Oregon with his wife Sylvia. He is an active member of the Portland poetry community, including two terms on the Oregon Poetry Association Board of Directors (OPA) and as a participant in several critique groups. He is an almost perpetual poetry student at the Attic Institute of Arts and Letters in Portland as a multi-year member of its Poets Studio and a 2016-17 Fellow of its Atheneum. His poetry has been published in three anthologies, *Port Chicago Poets, Terra Incognita* and *Matter II, Volume I,* two on line journals, *Brick and Mortar Review* and *Writersresist.com.* Two prize winning poems appeared in annual issues of the OPA *Verseweavers Anthology of Winning Poems.* A third prize winning poem will appear in the 2023 issue. His political poetry appeared in the chapbook, *The Covfefe Resistance.*

On *Telling Signs* by Marvin J. Lurie:

Voices draw me into this book, and voices keep me reading—voices of the dead in persona poems, voices in which the poet seems to speak directly. Many of the poems are compressed narratives, conveyed through a sequence of short, declarative sentences in end-stopped lines. The title poem, a reflective look at the life of a hunting/companion dog, is among these: "Walks became shorter / until she was content / with the living room rug and back yard / as her whole world." The flat presentation in such poems enhances the impact of the content by leaving room for readers' emotional responses. In several poems, though, the voice turns prophetic, indignant: "You who were seeded by the stars, / what have you done?" In the book's longest poem, the haunting "In the Garden," it is incantatory, weaving a spell through an intricate structure of repetition.

Taken together, the poems have a long perspective—personal, Biblical, archaeological. They are sensitive to injustice and incline to irony. The juxtaposition of voices from soldiers of the Old Testament and those of both Confederate and Union soldiers of the American Civil War makes manifest the randomness and unfairness of what happens in any war: "One army camp / can look like any other one."

The poet's Jewish heritage gives him a direct experience of the life-and-death difference that history can make for particular people. In "The Undesirables" we learn that his ancestors, "Rebekah and Jacob the tailor," came to the U.S. in 1905. Soon afterward, U.S. immigration laws became more restrictive. Left behind, "Jacob's younger sister, her husband and daughter, / were taken out of their home and shot down in the street / by the Einsatzgruppen."

In poem after poem, passionate indignation and rueful awareness are compacted into tightly written lines. The poet's testimony is the more trustworthy because he does not spare himself: "I discard the past, unprepared / for what might well up years later / to demand closure." Through these poems, he recovers and honors the past—multiple layers of the past—and implicitly acknowledges that there can be no closure.

Eleanor Berry
Past President, National Federation of State Poetry Societies
Author of *Works of Wildfire* and three earlier poetry collections.

www.ingramcontent.com/pod-product-compliance
Lightning Source LLC
Chambersburg PA
CBHW030224170426
43194CB00007BA/859